I'm Just Too Much

Audra DeRidder

Write and Release
PUBLISHING

www.writeandreleasepublishing.com

In honor of my grandfather, for
passing on his love of writing

To my daughter and my students;
sometimes being "too much" is the
best way to be.

My name is Sylvie J. and sometimes I'm just too much.

My 2nd grade teacher, Mr. Stanley, says sometimes I am just too much. Well, he doesn't say that to me, but I can tell by the way he shakes his head and lets out a sigh when I'm called on.

I try to sit in my chair, but sometimes I'm just too wiggly.

I try to wait and raise my hand, but
sometimes I am just too excited.

I try to be quiet, but sometimes my voice just comes
out too loud.

Sometimes, I'm just too much

I have the very best of friends you can have. Luca and Lilah, (yes they're twins) but sometimes I am too much for them too. Well they don't say that, but I can tell by the way they roll their eyes at me.

I try to go with the flow and play along, but sometimes I'm just too bossy.

I try to listen when they talk about their favorite things, but sometimes I'm just too chatty.

I try not to get upset when something happens, but sometimes I'm just too emotional.

And sometimes, when I'm just too much, my friends leave.

When I try not to be "too much", I end up feeling like nothing at all.

My voice gets too quiet and I don't talk.

My body gets too still and I don't move.

My brain gets too busy trying to keep me quiet and still, that it just won't do anything at all.

When my brain is "just too much" it reminds me that I always have new and creative ideas. Like making games, puzzles, art, and stories.

When my voice is "just too much" it reminds me that I can use it to make friends and say what I feel. Like telling my friends I care about them, and standing up for what is right.

When my body is "just too much" it reminds me that I am full of energy to play and to do the things I want to do. Like dancing, running, skipping and swinging.

When my emotions are "just too much" it reminds me that I can be passionate and feel the very best feelings. Like love, happiness, excitement and curiosity.

Sometimes being just too much is just the right amount after all.

CPSIA information can be obtained
at www.ICGtesting.com
Printed in the USA
LVHW072147230723
752884LV00008BA/90